HOW TO MASSAGE YOUR CAT

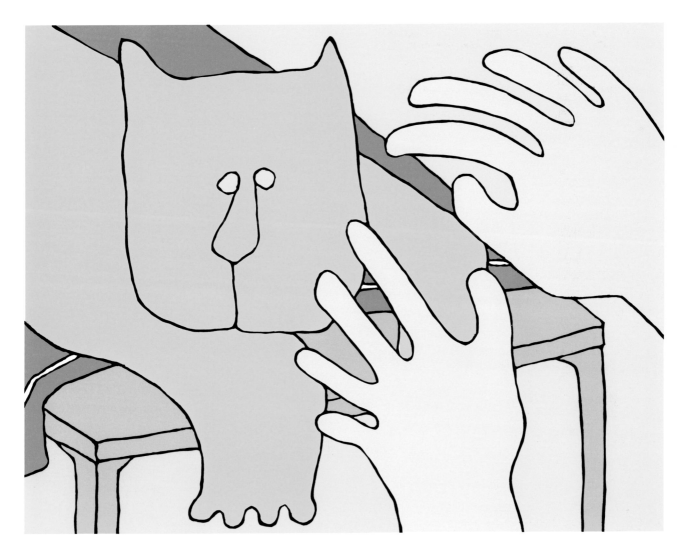

WRITTEN AND ILLUSTRATED BY ALICE M. BROCK

Chronicle Books   San Francisco

Printed in Hong Kong.

Library of Congress Cataloging-in-Publication Data:
Brock, Alice May, 1941-
How to massage your cat / by Alice M. Brock.
p. cm
Originally published: New York: Knopf, 1985.
ISBN: 0-8118-0203-5
1. Cats--Humor. I. Title.
PN6231.C23B76 1992
818' .5402--dc20   91-38171
                            CIP
Distributed in Canada by Raincoast Books,
112 East Third Avenue, Vancouver, B. C. V5T 1C8

10 9 8 7 6 5 4 3 2

Chronicle Books
275 Fifth St.
San Francisco, CA 94103.

FOR JOE

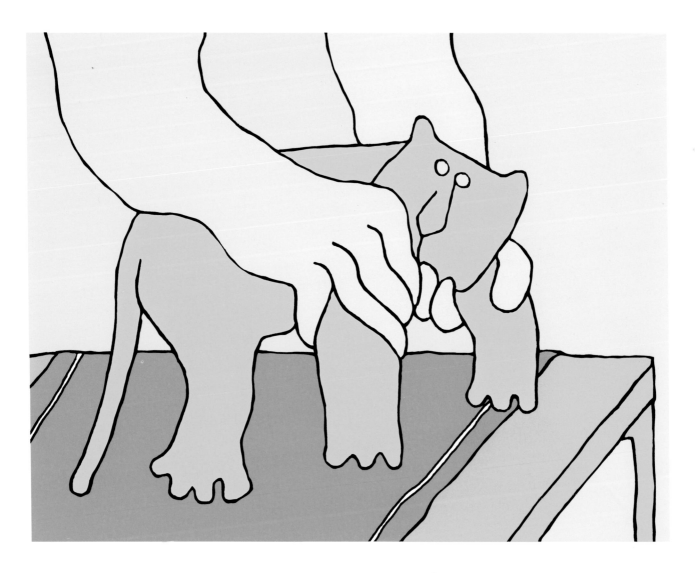

ARRANGE THE CAT NICELY ON A CLEAN TOWEL

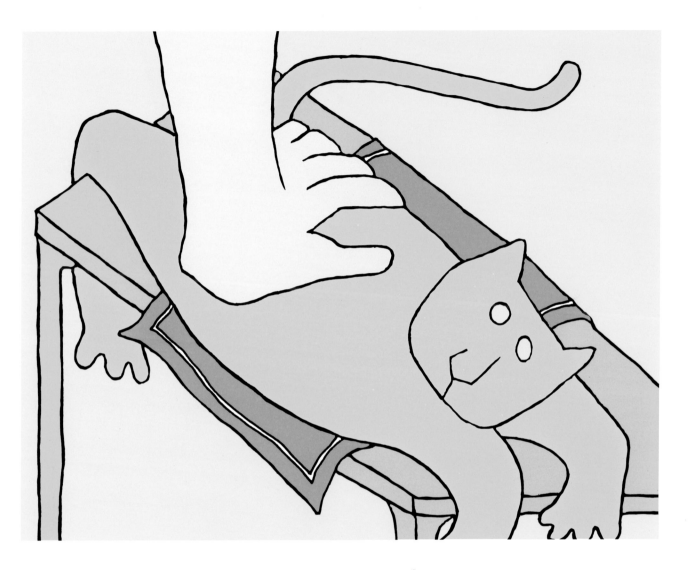

AND PRESS FIRMLY INTO PLACE

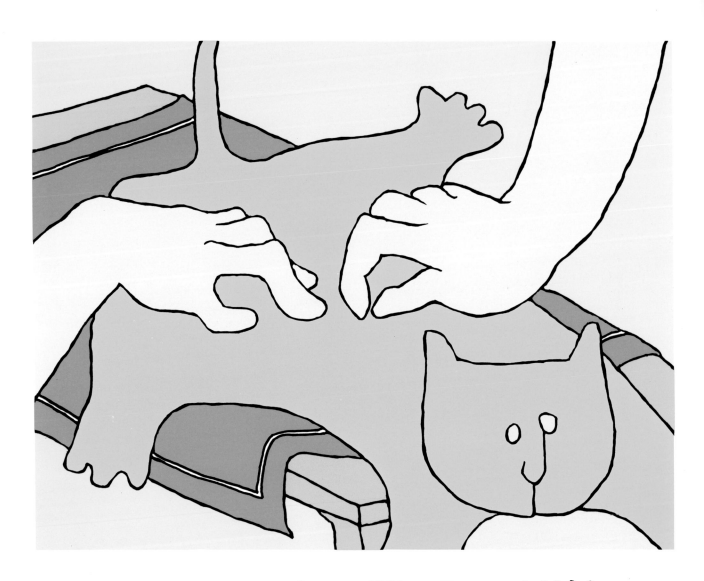

INSPECT CAT THOROUGHLY

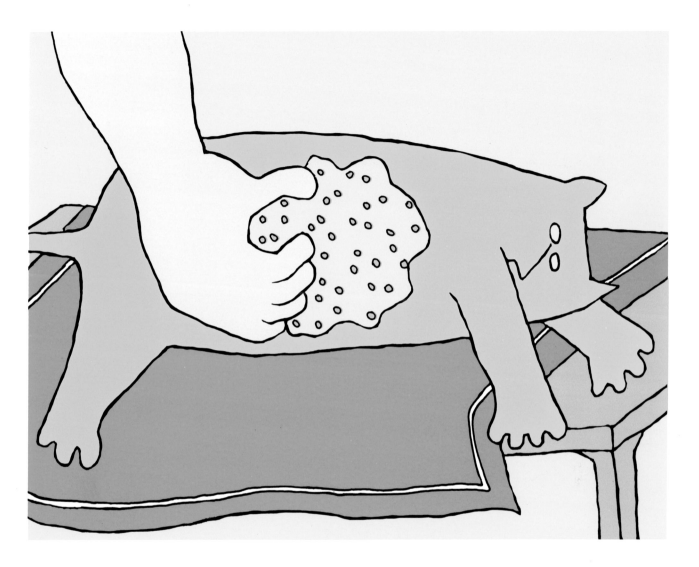

REMOVE ALL DEBRIS AND LOOSE HAIR
WITH A MOISTENED SPONGE

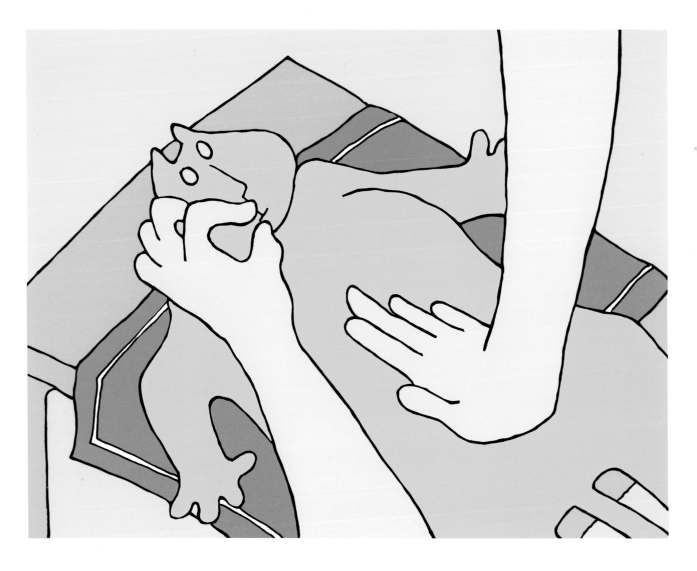

PINCH LIPS SHUT AND THRUST FINGERS UNDER RIBCAGE. AN AUDIBLE INTAKE OF BREATH WILL SIGNAL PROPER RESPIRATION HAS BEGUN

SET CAT UPRIGHT IN ITS NORMAL
SEATED POSITION

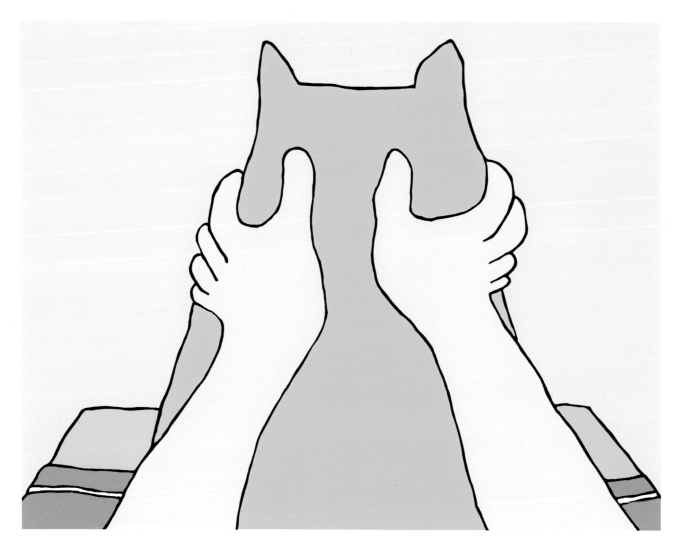

PLACE THUMBS BEHIND EARS AND
LOCK FINGERS SECURELY UNDER CHIN

RAISE CAT 8 TO 9 INCHES ABOVE TABLE
AND SHAKE ENERGETICALLY

THE CAT SHOULd FEEL COMPLETELY LOOSENEd

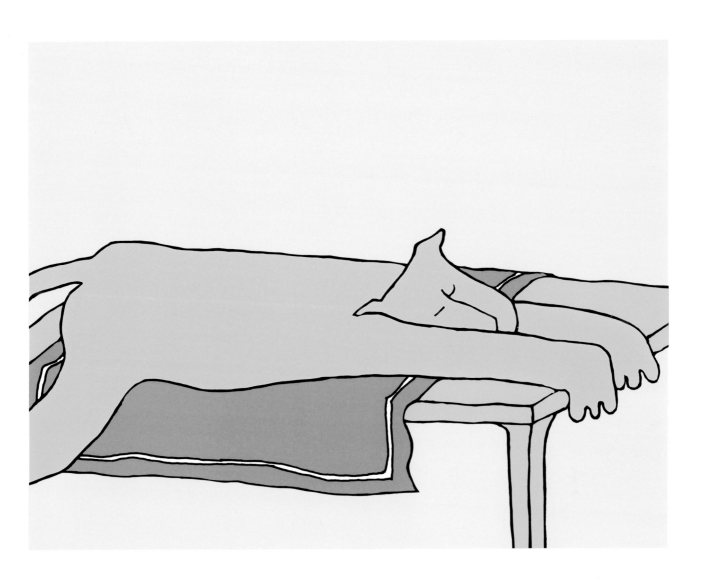

ALLOW CAT TO REST A MOMENT

APPROACH CAT QUIETLY WITH

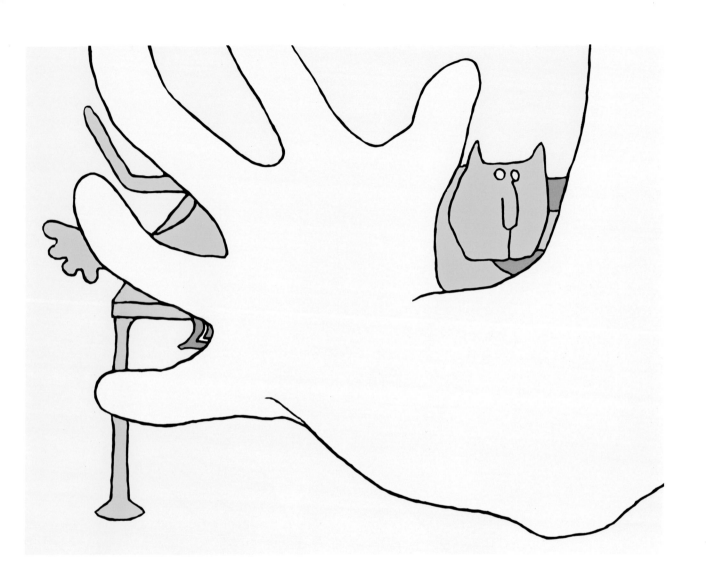

PALMS UP AND OPEN

BEGIN AT THE REAR

AND WORK YOUR WAY AROUND THE CAT
USING A VIGOROUS KNEADING MOTION

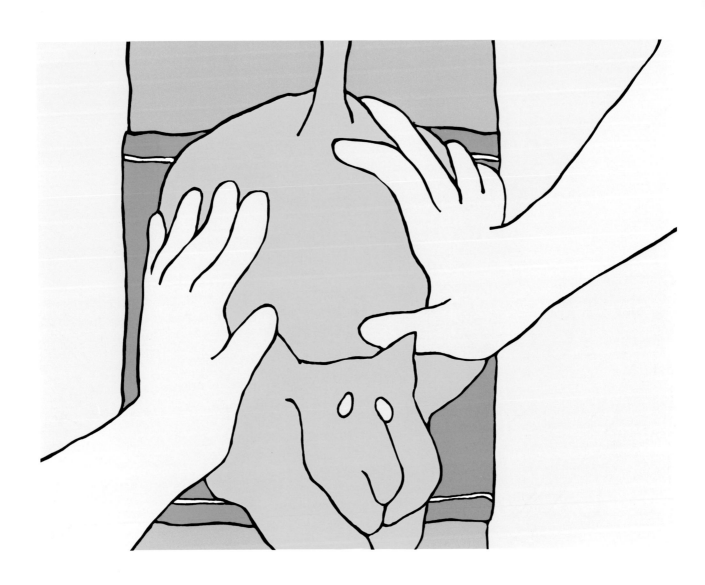

BUNCHiNG iT UP

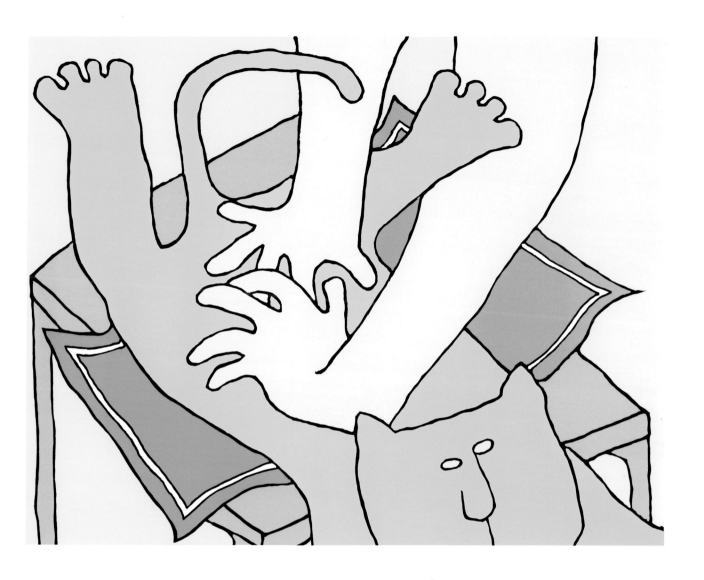

AND SPREADING IT OUT

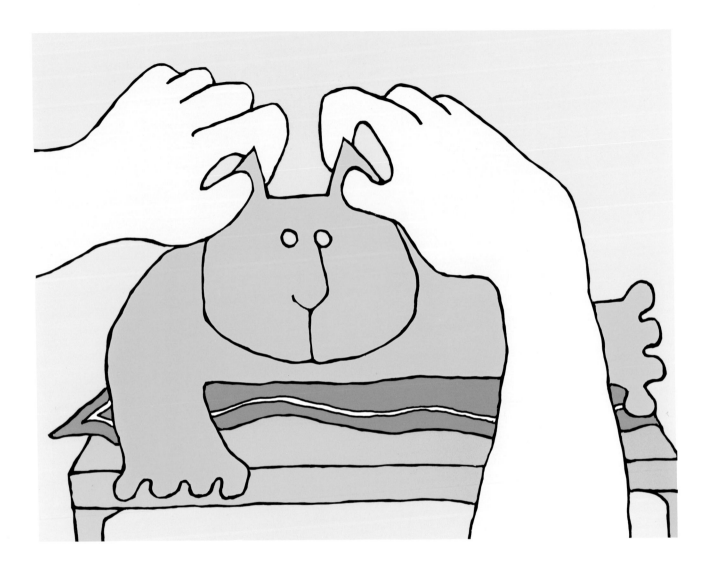

STAND SQUARELY IN FRONT OF CAT
AND GRASP IT BY BOTH EARS

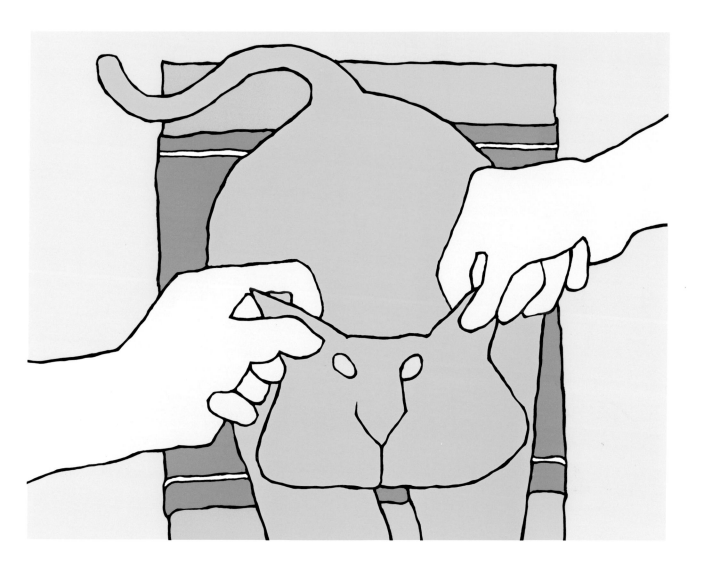

PRESS FIRMLY BACK TILL YOU HEAR
THE CLICK

NOW DRAW FRONT LEGS OUT AT RIGHT ANGLES TO THE BODY AND TUG SHARPLY

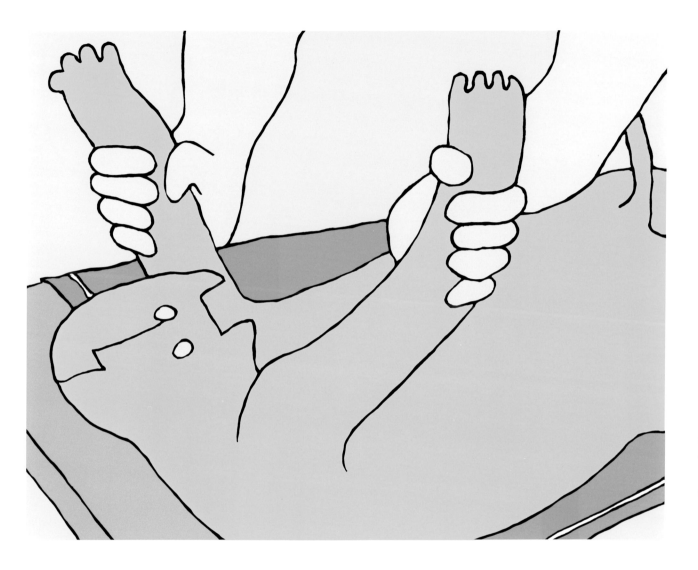

ROTATE FULLY EXTENDED LIMBS
UNTIL THEY RIDE FREE IN SOCKETS

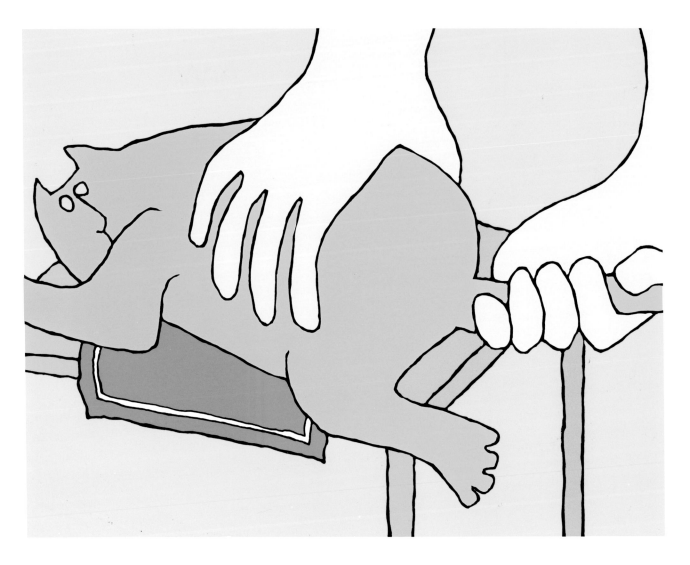

GRIP TAIL TIGHTLY AND TURN SLOWLY
COUNTERCLOCKWISE

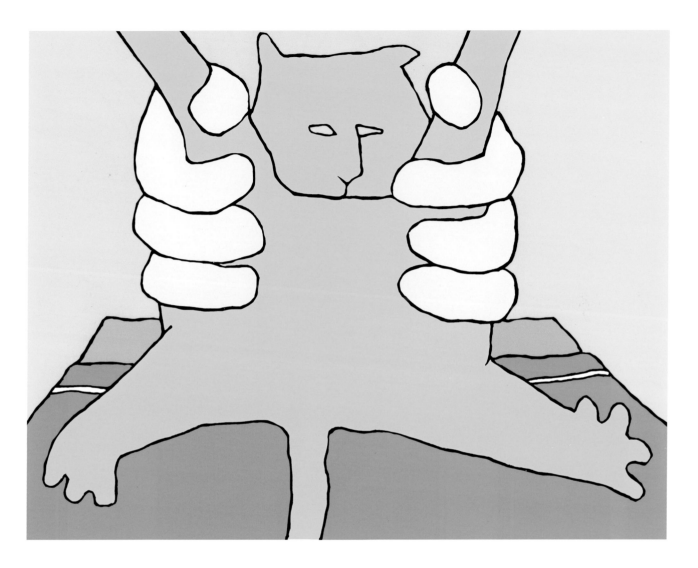

GENTLY FLIP CAT OVER ONTO ITS BACK

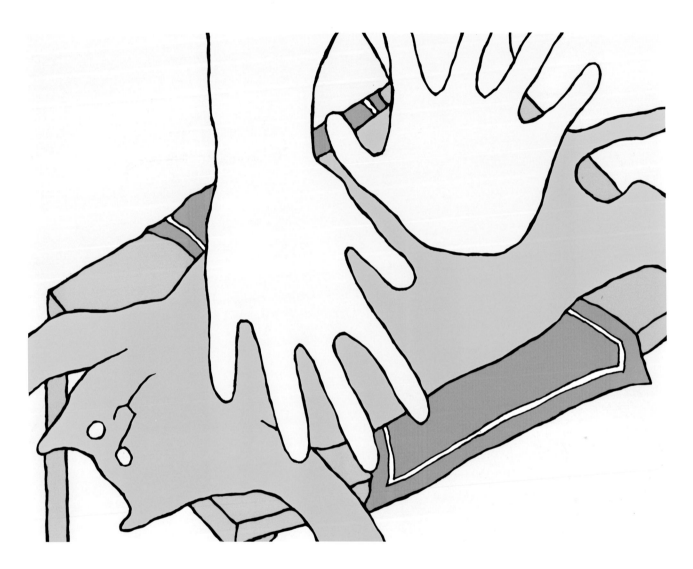

AND DIRECT A VOLLEY OF RAPID SLAPS
TO THE MIDRIFF

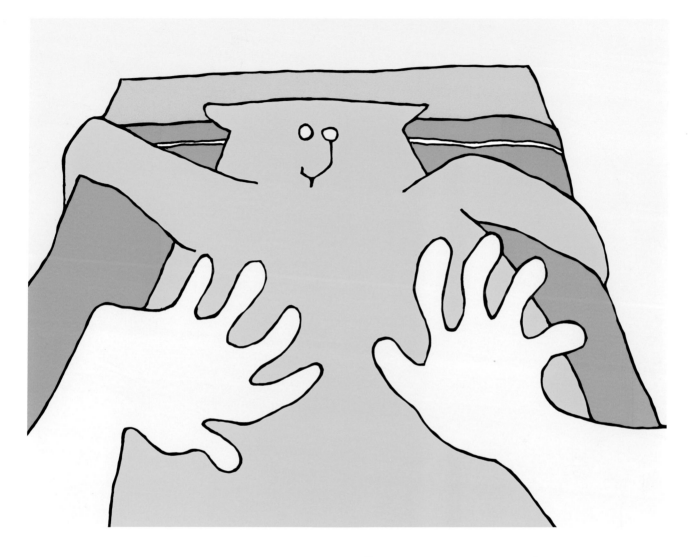

FINISH UP IMMEDIATELY WITH A
BRISK BODY RUB

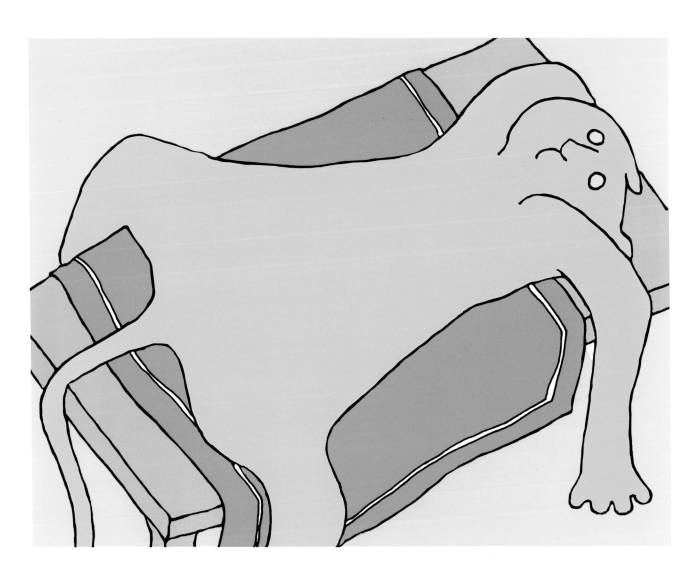

AT THIS POINT YOUR CAT SHOULD BE
ENTIRELY RELAXED

COVER THE FACE BRIEFLY WITH A
TEA TOWEL TO PROLONG CALM

A WELL MASSAGED CAT MAY REMAIN
IN THIS POSITION

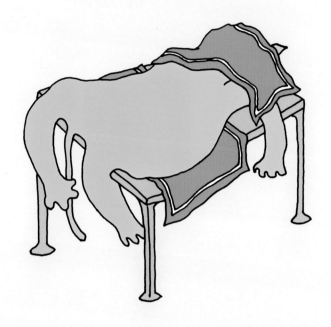

FOR SOME TIME